America's Latinos

A Proud Heritage The Hispanic Library

America's Latinos

Their Rich History, Culture, and Traditions

Julie Amparano

The Child's World

Published in the United States of America by The Child's World®
PO Box 326 • Chanhassen, MN 55317-0326 • 800-599-READ • www.childsworld.com

Acknowledgments
   The Creative Spark: Mary Francis-DeMarois, Project Director; Carrie Nichols Cantor, Series
   Editor; Robert Court, Design and Art Direction
   Carmen Blanco, Curriculum Adviser
   The Child's World®: Mary Berendes, Publishing Director

Photos
   AFP/CORBIS: 32; Rod Aydelotte/Waco Tribune Herald: 17; Richard Bickel/Corbis: 13;
   Bettmann/CORBIS: 29, 34; Phil Cantor: 31; Early American Digital Library: 9; Walter
   Hodges/CORBIS: 14; Library of Congress: 9, 11, 18, 30; Kelly-Mooney Photography/CORBIS:
   cover; Lucy Nicholson/AFP/CORBIS: 33; Sam Mercovich/Reuters NewsMedia Inc./CORBIS:
   35; Star Ledger: 20, 22, 25, 30; Texas Department of Transportation: 19, 26; University of
   Virginia, Alderman Library: 7

Library of Congress Cataloging-in-Publication Data
   Amparano, Julie.
     America's Latinos : their rich history, culture, and traditions / by Julie Amparano.
         p. cm. — (A proud heritage : the Hispanic library)
   Summary: Introduces the history, culture, and customs of America's Latinos.
   Includes bibliographical references and index.
   Contents: The Spanish come to America — Different homelands and
   cultures — Part of the American fabric — Famous Hispanic Americans.
     ISBN 1-56766-083-5 (lib. bdg. : alk. paper)
    1. Hispanic Americans—Juvenile literature. [1. Hispanic Americans.]
   I. Title. II. Series: Proud heritage (Child's World (Firm)
   E184.S75 A826 2003
   973'.0468—dc21

                                    2002151724

Contents

9   17   26   30

Chapter One

The Spanish Come to America

Latinos have a long history in the United States. It is even longer than that of the English Pilgrims who landed at Plymouth Rock in 1620. Most Latinos, also known as Hispanics, are the **descendants** of Spanish colonists and Native Americans. Some also have African origins.

The Spanish Explorers

It all began when Spain "discovered" America in 1492. Spain's king and queen paid for the famous **expedition** led by Christopher Columbus (who was actually from Italy). Columbus expected to sail west to China and India. His journey across the ocean was long and dangerous. He sailed for more than two months where no one had ever gone. When he landed on the islands in the Caribbean Sea, he claimed them for Spain. He called the people he saw Indians because he thought he was in

India. (Today they are known as Native Americans.) Columbus died in 1506, never realizing he had found a whole new continent.

The first Spanish explorer to reach what is now U.S. soil was Juan Ponce de León. He is famous for

This old map shows what Europeans thought North America looked like in 1571. You can see that they did not realize how large the American continent was or how far it extended to the west. Notice how close they thought India was. "Die Nüw Welt" is German for "The New World."

discovering Florida. Ponce de León had arrived with Columbus on his second voyage to North America in 1493. He later became the governor of the island now called Puerto Rico. Native Americans told him of an island called Bimini that had gold, pearls, and the magical Fountain of Youth.

In 1513, Ponce de León went searching for Bimini. He thought he found it when he landed in what is now Florida. He claimed the land for Spain and named it Pascua de Florida, which means "feast of flowers." Finding no treasure and no Fountain of Youth, Ponce de León returned home.

Other Spanish explorers who traveled through what is now the United States were Francisco Vásquez de Coronado and Hernando de Soto. Both launched major expeditions in search of the Seven Cities of Cíbola, which were said to be full of treasure.

In August 1540, Coronado and 1,000 men set out from central Mexico and went north to hunt for the cities of gold. They spent nearly three years searching for riches in the region that is now the states of Arizona, New Mexico, Texas, Oklahoma, and Kansas. Along the way they discovered the Grand Canyon, the Great Bend, and the Rio Grande. Coronado reached the area that was thought to be Cíbola (in New Mexico), but it turned out to be just a region of poor villages.

This engraving shows Hernando de Soto sailing off from Spain to conquer Florida.

Coronado returned to Mexico City in 1542. Only 100 men came back with him. During their travels, they conquered and killed many Native Americans. Historians say Coronado covered more territory in a shorter period of time than any other Spanish explorer. He claimed the desert lands for Spain and paved the way for people to settle what is now known as the American Southwest.

De Soto launched an expedition from Cuba in 1539 with 600 men. Over the next four years, de Soto's men marched through regions of forests and prairies. They explored much of what is now Georgia, South Carolina, Alabama, Mississippi, Arkansas, and Louisiana. Like Coronado, de Soto was searching for the Seven Cities of Cíbola. De Soto and nearly half of his men died searching for treasure. They, too, killed many Native Americans along the way.

These early Spanish explorers had a great influence on America. They founded two of its earliest cities: Saint Augustine, Florida, in 1565; and Santa Fe, New Mexico, in 1598. They gave Spanish names to hundreds of U.S. rivers, mountains, towns, and even several states. *Colorado,* the name given to a state with vast areas of red rock, is Spanish for "colored red." *Los Angeles* means "the angels."

Spanish Settlers

After the expeditions, some Spanish people came to live in small settlements across the South and Southwest. Some were military forts and others were Catholic **missions.** The missions were beautiful structures built in a square around a garden. They had many graceful arches. The **missionaries** wanted to teach the Native Americans Christianity, farming, and the European way of life. Many of the mission buildings still exist, and people today enjoy visiting them.

Many Spaniards settled down and made families with Native Americans. Their children were known as **mestizos,**

The dramatic meeting of two different cultures, that of the Spanish and that of the Native Americans, forever changed the Americas.

or people who are half Spanish and half Native American. Most Hispanics today are descendants of those mestizo families. Later, Spaniards would create families with African slaves in other places, such as Cuba and Puerto Rico.

New U.S. Lands

Many other Hispanics became U.S. citizens as the new country took over more land. In 1836, Texas, which was part of Mexico, fought for its independence from Mexico. In 1845, it became the 28th state of the United States.

In 1846, the United States and Mexico went to war because the United States wanted more land. Mexico lost and was forced to sell the northern half of its territory to the United States. The lands now known as California, Utah, and Nevada as well as parts of Colorado, Wyoming, New Mexico, and Arizona were no longer part of Mexico.

Then, in 1898, the United States took control of Puerto Rico as part of the **treaty** that ended the Spanish-American War. Many of the people living in these new American territories later became U.S. citizens.

Immigration

Since the 1800s, many Mexicans, as well as other Latin Americans, have immigrated to the United States.

This picture shows three Mexicans floating on a raft across the Rio Grande River to try to enter the United States illegally. About 4.5 million illegal immigrants from Mexico live in the United States.

Another large group of Hispanics came from Cuba in the 1960s and '70s, when Cubans fled their country's **communist** government.

Today, the U.S. Latino community continues to grow, as people from Mexico and other parts of Latin America leave their homelands to find a better way of life in the United States. Some are so eager to live here that they risk arrest and even death to come illegally.

Hispanics are expected to make up 20 percent of the U.S. population by the year 2020.

Latinos soon will be the largest minority group in the United States. Today they represent 13 percent of the total U.S. population. By the year 2020, one out of every five Americans will be of Hispanic descent.

As we have seen, Hispanics do not come from one nation, race, or culture. Yet, they are related by their Spanish history, language, and many shared customs. In the next chapter, we will see that Latinos in the United States come from many places and have brought with them the customs and traditions of their many different homelands.

Where Hispanics Live in the United States

Hispanics live in almost every part of the United States. But 83 percent of them are found in only ten states. They are:

California: 12.1 million	**Arizona:** 1.5 million
Texas: 7.3 million	**New Jersey:** 1.2 million
Florida: 3.1 million	**Colorado:** 838,000
New York: 3 million	**New Mexico:** 797,000
Illinois: 1.7 million	**Georgia:** 487,000

(From Strategy Corporation's *2002 U.S. Hispanic Market Report*)

Chapter Two

Different Homelands and Cultures

The three largest Hispanic groups in the United States are Mexican Americans, Puerto Ricans, and Cuban Americans. Many others come from the Dominican Republic and various countries in Central and South America. What are these places like, and why did so many people leave them to come to the United States?

Mexico

Mexico today is a nation of 100 million people. It lies south of the United States. Its name was derived from Mexítli, the Aztec god of war. Most Mexicans speak Spanish, though many Mexican Native Americans also speak their native languages. English is becoming more and more popular across the country, especially in cities.

The descendants of Mexicans who live in the United States are known as Mexican Americans or Chicanos.

About 20 million people of Mexican heritage live in the United States. They are the largest group of Hispanics in the United States.

Native American tribes lived in the area now called Mexico for thousands of years before the arrival of

Young girls perform Mexican folk dances.

the Spaniards in 1519. Mexico was ruled by Spain and was called New Spain for 300 years. The country of Mexico was founded in 1821, after an 11-year war of independence against Spain. Mexico used to be about twice as large as it is now, but it lost much of its land to the United States after the Mexican War.

Mexico is not a rich country. Many Mexican workers earn in one day what workers in the United States earn in one hour. Because the country is so poor, many Mexicans travel to the United States to find better jobs to support their families. Hundreds die each year trying to cross the border illegally. In most cases, they either drown trying

Here is a photo of a Mexican man with his donkey in Nuevo Laredo, Mexico, around 1912. He is moving to the United States, as have many Mexicans over the years.

to cross a river or die of heat and thirst in the desert. On average, one person dies each day trying to cross the U.S.-Mexico border.

Puerto Rico

Puerto Rico is an island south of Florida in the Caribbean Sea. It is a U.S. **commonwealth.** That means it is part of

Mexicans are known for mariachi music, a style of music that dates back to the 1800s. Mariachi bands include guitar, violin, and trumpet. The lively music is often played at special occasions, such as weddings and birthday parties. The mariachi players dress in flashy charro suits, which are formal cowboy vests and pants. You can enjoy their music in many Mexican restaurants around the United States.

Traditional folk music in Puerto Rico is a blend of the island's Spanish, African, and Taíno traditions. People all over the world love salsa music. Salsa was first played by Puerto Rican musicians living in New York City in the 1950s and '60s. The popular dance music draws heavily on Cuban and Afro-Caribbean sounds.

The boy is watching the annual Puerto Rican parade in Newark, New Jersey. He is draped in the Puerto Rican flag.

the United States but is not a state like Texas or California.

Puerto Ricans are U.S. citizens. They can travel freely from the island to the U.S. mainland. Some Puerto Ricans would like their island to become the 51st state.

Nearly 4 million people live in Puerto Rico. Most speak Spanish, although English is taught in the island's schools. Puerto Ricans are descendants of Spanish settlers, African slaves, and the native Taínos.

About 3.5 million Puerto Ricans live in the 50 states of the United States. Puerto Ricans are the second largest group of Latinos in the United States. Most Puerto Ricans who live on the mainland are in New York City, Chicago, New Jersey, and Florida.

Before it became a U.S. commonwealth, Puerto Rico was a Spanish colony. Puerto Ricans tried for many years to win independence from Spain, beginning in 1868. They did not succeed. Then, in 1898, the United States took Puerto Rico after defeating Spain.

Cuba

Cuba is a tropical island nation located only 90 miles (145 kilometers) off the coast of Florida in the Caribbean Sea. It is the largest country in the Caribbean. About 11 million people live in Cuba. Most Cubans are descendants of Spaniards and African slaves.

Food, Glorious Food

Many popular foods now enjoyed in the United States came from Mexico, including tortillas, which are made from flour or ground corn; salsa, which is usually a spicy tomato sauce; and chocolate.

Puerto Rican cooking is similar to Spanish and Mexican cooking. It combines Spanish, African, Taíno, and American influences. Puerto Ricans call their cuisine cocina criolla.

Typical Cuban food includes black beans and rice, fried sliced banana, garlic marinades, rice dishes, and boiled yucca (a root vegetable similar to a potato).

This Cuban woman holds one flag from her native country and one flag from her adopted country.

The island was colonized by Spain in 1511 and became an independent country in 1901. Cuba became a communist nation in 1959. President Fidel Castro has ruled the country ever since. Communism is a form of government that does not allow people to freely elect their leaders.

Many older Cuban Americans moved to the United States in the 1960s after Castro took power. By 1963, more than 200,000 people had left Cuba and come to the United States. About 1.5 million people of Cuban origin live in the United States today.

Miami, Florida, is considered the center of Cuban American life. There also are many Cuban Americans in the states of New Jersey, New York, and Illinois.

The Dominican Republic

The Dominican Republic is another island in the Caribbean that was once a Spanish colony. Today it is a very poor country.

More than 800,000 Hispanics in the United States trace their roots to the Dominican Republic. Most of them live in New York City.

Central and South America

Central America includes seven nations just south of Mexico and north of Colombia. They are Belize, Costa Rica, El Salvador, Guatemala, Honduras, Nicaragua, and Panama.

Until the 1980s, fewer than 100,000 Central Americans lived in the United States. Then wars in the countries of El Salvador, Nicaragua, and Guatemala in the 1980s and '90s forced many people to leave the region. Nearly 2 million people whose roots can be traced to Central America now live in the United States.

Hispanics who came from South American lands account for about 2.5 million people in the United States. In South America there are 13 countries. They are Argentina, Bolivia, Brazil, Chile, Colombia, Ecuador, French Guiana, Guyana, Venezuela, Paraguay, Peru, Surinam, and Uruguay.

Chapter Three

Part of the American Fabric

Latinos have left behind neither their cultures nor their customs. In fact, they have woven parts of their heritage into the American fabric.

Many Latinos live in *barrios,* or Spanish-speaking neighborhoods. One of the best known is Spanish Harlem in New York City. In Miami, there is the famous Calle Ocho. In Los Angeles, there is lively Olvera Street and its amazing **bazaar.** The barrio residents celebrate their heritage with parades and festivals throughout the year.

Even outside the barrios, Latino culture can be seen everywhere. Turn on the radio and listen to the words of the latest pop songs. Spanish words and phrases are common. Ricky Martin's 2000 hit "Livin' La Vida Loca" is one example. President George W. Bush even danced to the tune with Martin during his inaugural celebration. Richie Valens's recording of "La Bamba" entirely in

Spanish was a big hit in the United States in the 1950s. The song is still played today. Other Spanish songs that have become popular in the United States are "Cielito Lindo," "La Cucaracha," and "Guantanamera."

Ricky Martin performs at Madison Square Garden in New York City in 1999.

Language

The Spanish language has become part of America's everyday vocabulary. People use Spanish words and phrases all the time. We call our friends *amigos.* We say good-bye with an *adios* or an *hasta la vista.* And don't we all love to take an afternoon *siesta?*

Most Americans don't even realize how many cities, rivers, mountains, and other landmarks have Spanish names. *Rio Grande* means "large river." *San Antonio* translates into "Saint Anthony." The list continues with Las Vegas, San Diego, San Francisco, Nevada, Santa Fe, Sacramento, and El Paso.

These Mexican-American family members have gathered together at a tamalada, *a traditional tamale-making party.*

Latino Food

Latino culture is also alive in the foods we eat. We enjoy tortillas, burritos, tacos, enchiladas, rice and beans, and guacamole. These dishes are so common that many non-Hispanics regularly make them at home. Americans now buy more bottles of salsa than ketchup.

And salsa is not just something to dip chips in. It is also an exciting form of music that many Americans have come to love. Salsa is a vibrant combination of rhythms from the African, Caribbean, and Latin regions of the world. The beats are quick and jazzy. Tejano and conjunto music also are popular. Tejano uses electric guitars and synthesizers and has a more electric sound. Conjunto has more of a folk guitar sound.

History

Latinos have contributed more than just food, language, and culture to the United States. They have played a role in the founding of the country. During the Revolutionary War, General Bernardo de Galvez, who was governor of the Louisiana Territory, sent money and supplies to George Washington to help him fight the British. Captain Jorge Farragut came to the United States from Spain to fight in the Revolutionary War.

Ever since, American Latinos have served proudly in war. In the Civil War (1861–1865), Commander David Glasgow Farragut, son of Jorge Farragut, became a hero for capturing the entire Gulf Coast for the Union. For bravery during the war, President Abraham Lincoln promoted him to rear admiral, making him the navy's highest-ranking officer. Many monuments and memorials were built in his honor.

Latinos also proved themselves during World War II (1939–1945). More than 400,000 Latinos fought in that conflict. They were awarded more medals than any other ethnic group.

Today, Latinos are contributing in all areas of society. They are sure to play an even larger role in the future growth and development of the United States.

Chapter Four

Famous Hispanic Americans

Christina Aguilera is one of today's hottest stars.

Some famous Latinos, such as Ricky Martin and Jennifer Lopez, have become household names. There are many other Hispanics who have done great things in America. Hispanics have been important in civil rights, politics, sports, entertainment, science, and other fields. Here are the stories of just a few of them.

Christina Aguilera: Pop Star

Christina Aguilera was born in Staten Island, New York, in 1980. Her father was from Ecuador. At age 12, Aguilera joined the cast of *The New Mickey Mouse Club,* appearing with future stars Britney Spears and Justin Timberlake of 'N Sync. In 1998, RCA Records signed Aguilera to her first record contract. Her first album included the hit singles "Genie in a Bottle" and "Come On Over Baby." She won Best New Artist at the 1990 Grammy Awards. Aguilera has been a success in both the English- and Spanish-language music scenes.

Luis Walter Alvarez: Scientist

Luis Walter Alvarez (1911–1988) was awarded the Nobel Prize for physics in 1968. He had helped design a ground-controlled radar system for landing aircraft. Alvarez is also known for his theory on why dinosaurs became extinct. Alvarez believed a meteorite struck the earth and cooled its climate, causing the dinosaurs to die out.

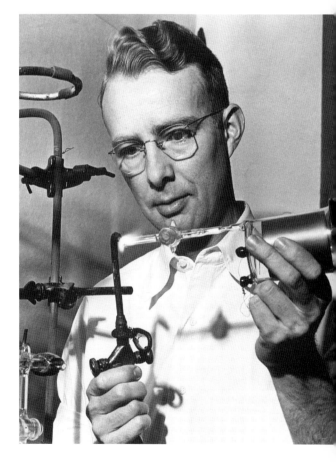

Luis Walter Alvarez won the Nobel Prize for physics.

César Chávez was a strong and courageous man who made a major contribution to social justice and civil rights in America.

César Chávez: Civil Rights Leader

César Chávez, a Mexican American, was born in Arizona in 1927 but later moved to California. He had to quit school after graduating from eighth grade and take a job picking grapes. It was there that Chávez first saw the horrible conditions migrant farm workers faced each day. Migrant farm families moved from town to town, picking crops. Their hours were long and their pay barely enough to live on. They had no rights. Many were forced to work with poisonous chemicals.

In 1962, Chávez and Dolores Huerta formed a union to help field-workers. Over the next several years, Chávez organized many strikes to try to force farm owners to do better for their workers. He had many successes. After meeting with Chávez, President John F. Kennedy called the labor leader "one of the heroic figures of our time." Chávez died in 1993. President Clinton awarded him the Medal of Freedom the following year.

Henry Cisneros: Politician

Henry Cisneros was the first Hispanic American to be elected mayor of a major American city when he became San Antonio's mayor in 1981. He later served in President Clinton's cabinet as Secretary of Housing and Urban Development.

Henry Cisneros was the first Hispanic mayor of a major American city.

Roberto Clemente: Hall of Fame Baseball Player and Humanitarian

Roberto Clemente was born in Puerto Rico in 1934. He spent most of his baseball career with the Pittsburgh Pirates. Clemente won four batting titles and was voted the National League's most valuable player (MVP) in 1966. After the 1972 season, Clemente was thinking about retiring.

In December 1972, a massive earthquake rocked the small Central American country of Nicaragua. Many people died or were left homeless. Clemente organized a relief effort and volunteered to fly food and medical supplies to Nicaragua himself. Tragically, his plane crashed just off the

Celia Cruz is the Queen of Salsa.

shore of Puerto Rico. His body was never found. He was 38 years old. Three months later, Clemente was inducted into the Baseball Hall of Fame.

Celia Cruz: Salsa Singer

Cuban-born singer Celia Cruz moved to the United States in 1960 to perform with Tito Puente and other great jazz and salsa artists in New York City. Cruz has recorded more than 70 albums and has appeared in several movies. She is known as the Queen of Salsa.

Jaime Escalante: Educator

Jaime Escalante was born in Bolivia but moved to the United States in 1964. Escalante taught math at Garfield High School in Los Angeles in 1976 to poor black and Hispanic students who were not expected to do well. He got a small group of students to take and pass the advanced placement (college-level) calculus exam in 1982. But the scores were thrown out because the people grading the test assumed the students had cheated. Most of the students retook the test and passed. The story inspired the 1988 movie *Stand and Deliver*. President Clinton awarded Escalante the Medal of Freedom.

Dolores Huerta: Civil Rights Leader

Mexican American Dolores Huerta was born in 1930 in New Mexico, where her father was a miner and a state assemblyman. She and César Chávez founded the United Farm Workers of America to improve the lives of farm workers. Dolores was inducted into the National Women's Hall of Fame in 1993 for her lifetime commitment to civil and human rights

Jennifer Lopez: Actress, Singer, and Dancer

Born in 1970 in the Bronx, New York, Jennifer Lopez is one of the highest-paid and best-known actresses in Hollywood. J.Lo, as she is known, started out as a dancer. She was one of the first Flygirls on the hit show *In Living Color*. Her first major film role was the lead in *Selena* (1997), the story of a singer killed by the head of her fan club. Lopez went on to star in a number of other films. Somehow, she also found time for a recording career, scoring many hits. Lopez's family comes from Puerto Rico.

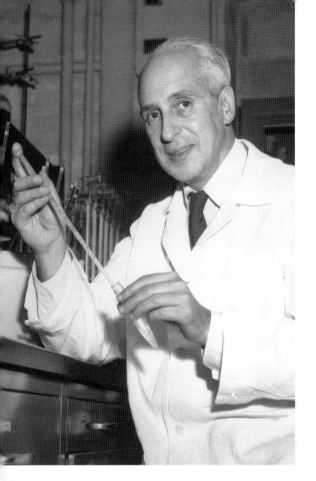

Dr. Severo Ochoa won the Nobel Prize in medicine.

Dr. Severo Ochoa: Scientist

Dr. Severo Ochoa (1905–1993) won the Nobel Prize for medicine in 1959. He helped discover RNA, one of the building blocks of life. Born in Spain, Ochoa became an American citizen in 1956.

Tito Puente: Percussionist

They called Tito Puente the King of Latin Music and the Mambo King. Puente was born in 1923 in East Harlem, New York, to Puerto Rican parents. During his 60-year career, Puente won five Grammy Awards, appeared in many movies, and was awarded a star on the Hollywood Walk of Fame. His hit records have become classics around the world. Puente recorded more than 100 albums and helped define Latin jazz and salsa. He died in 2000.

Carlos Santana: Rock Guitarist

Carlos Santana began his life in Mexico. His father was a violin player in a traditional mariachi band. More than 50 years later, Carlos Santana has sold more than 50 million albums. His musical style includes jazz, rock, Latin, blues, and pop. Santana was inducted into the Rock and Roll Hall of Fame in 1998. His album *Supernatural* won nine awards at the 2000 Grammy Awards.

Martin Sheen: Actor

Martin Sheen's real name is Ramon Estevez. He was born in Dayton, Ohio, in 1940, one of ten children of a Spanish immigrant father and an Irish mother. He chose the stage name Martin Sheen when he became an actor. Sheen has appeared in many movies. He is best known for playing the president of the United States in the television show *The West Wing*.

Martin Sheen is a successful film and television actor.

From music and sports to civil rights and science, America's Latinos have contributed to every aspect of U.S. society. Their rich history, culture, and traditions are a vital part of the past, present, and future of the United States of America.

1493: Juan Ponce de León accompanies Christopher Columbus on his second voyage. They land at the Virgin Islands and Puerto Rico.

1509: Juan Ponce de León settles on the island of San Juan Bautista, now known as Puerto Rico, after conquering the Native American population.

1513: Juan Ponce de León explores Florida.

1539: Hernando de Soto explores the area now known as Florida, Mississippi, Tennessee, North Carolina, Arkansas, and Louisiana, while searching for the Seven Golden Cities of Cíbola.

1540: Francisco Vásquez de Coronado launches an expedition through present-day Arizona, New Mexico, Texas, Oklahoma, and Kansas. He is also searching for the Seven Golden Cities of Cíbola.

1565: Saint Augustine, Florida, is founded by Pedro Menéndez de Avilés. The city is the oldest permanent European settlement in the United States.

1598: Juan de Oñate begins colonizing New Mexico.

1691: Father Eusebio Kino makes his first missionary inroad into Arizona.

1769: Father Junípero Serra arrives in San Diego, California, and establishes first California mission.

1821: The United States buys Florida from Spain for $5 million.

Mexico wins its independence from Spain after an 11-year war.

1822: Joseph Marion Hernandez becomes the first Latino elected to the U.S. Congress.

1836: Texas declares its independence from Mexico.

1845: Texas joins the United States as the 28th state.

1848: The United States defeats Mexico in war, bringing into the union territories that form the present states of Arizona, New Mexico, California, Nevada, and Utah, and parts of Colorado, Oklahoma, and Wyoming.

1898: The United States declares war against Spain and, as a result of its victory, comes to own Puerto Rico, the Virgin Islands, the Philippines, and Guam and occupies Cuba for two years.

1910: The Mexican Revolution begins. Many Mexicans take refuge in the United States.

1928: Octaviano A. Larrazolo becomes the first Latino elected to the U.S. Senate.

1959: Fidel Castro leads a revolution in Cuba ousting dictator Fulgencio Batista. Over the next several years, hundreds of thousands of Cubans flee to the United States.

Dr. Severo Ochoa wins the Nobel Prize for medicine.

1962: Edward R. Roybal is elected to serve in the U.S. Congress.

César Chávez and Dolores Huerta form the United Farm Workers union.

1965: César Chávez and the United Farm Workers union launch a series of strikes against growers.

1968: Luis Walter Alvarez wins the Nobel Prize for physics.

1981: Henry Cisneros becomes the first Hispanic elected mayor of a major U.S. city, San Antonio.

1988: President Reagan appoints Lauro Cavasos as secretary of education.

1993: President Clinton appoints two Hispanics to his cabinet, former mayors Henry Cisneros and Federico Peña.

2001: President Bush appoints Antonio González to serve as chief White House legal counsel.

bazaar (buh-ZAR) A bazaar is a street or marketplace filled with shops and stalls. Many Mexican neighborhoods in the United States have wonderful bazaars.

commonwealth (KOM-en-welth) A commonwealth is a self-governing political body that is voluntarily part of a larger country. The island of Puerto Rico is a U.S. commonwealth.

communist (KOM-yuh-nist) A communist is an advocate or supporter of communism, which is a form of government. A communist government is a dictatorship, not a democracy, and has complete control over wages, prices, and many other aspects of people's lives.

descendants (deh-SEN-dantz) Descendants are people born of a certain ancestor, family, or group. Some of today's Latinos are descendants of the Spanish explorers and missionaries who arrived centuries ago.

expedition (eks-puh-DISH-un) An expedition is a journey or voyage or march for some specific purpose, such as to explore or fight a war. Coronado led an expedition to search for gold north of Mexico.

mestizos (meh-STEE-zohs) Mestizos are people in the Spanish colonies who had Spanish and Native American parents. Many Spanish colonialists settled down with Native American women. Their children were mestizos.

missionaries (MISH-uh-neh-reez) Missionaries are people who teach their religion in other countries. Spain sent missionaries to teach the Native Americans about Christianity and the Catholic Church. They also taught the Native Americans to speak, read, and write Spanish.

missions (MIH-shuns) Missions were religious communities set up by Spanish Catholic church leaders. Missions would typically be built near small towns or forts.

treaty (TREE-tee) A treaty is a formal agreement between two or more countries. Treaties usually address peace or trade between the countries.

Books

Carter, Alden. *The Mexican War.* New York: Franklin Watts, 1992.

Catalano, Julie. *The Mexican Americans.* New York: Chelsea House, 1988.

Mohr, Nicholasa. *All for the Better: A Story of El Barrio.* Austin, Tex.: Raintree/Steck-Vaughn, 1996.

Nickles, Greg. *The Hispanics: We Came to North America.* New York: Crabtree, 2000.

Novas, Himilce. *Everything You Need to Know about Latino History.* New York: Plume, 1998.

Sinnott, Susan. *Extraordinary Hispanic Americans.* Chicago: Children's Press, 1991.

Web Sites

Visit our Web page for lots of links about America's Latinos:
http://www.childsworld.com/links.html

Note to parents, teachers, and librarians: We routinely monitor our Web links to make sure they're safe, active sites.

Sources Used by the Author

Bean, Frank D., and Marta Tienda. *The Hispanic Population of the United States.* New York: Russell Sage Foundation, 1988.

Fernández-Shaw, Carlos. *The Hispanic Presence in North America from 1941 to Today.* New York: Facts On File, 1987.

Gann, L.H., and Peter J. Duignan. *The Hispanics in the United States.* Boulder, Colo.: Westview Press. 1986.

Gonzalez, Juan. *Harvest of Empire: A History of Latinos in America.* New York: Viking Penguin. 2000.

Kanellos, Nicolás, with Cristelia Pérez. *Chronology of Hispanic-American History: From Pre-Columbian Times to the Present.* Detroit, Mich.: Gale Research Inc., 1995.

Novas, Himilce. *Everything You Need to Know about Latino History.* New York: Plume, 1998.

Shorris, Earl. *Latinos: A Biography of the People.* New York: W. W. Norton, 1992.